Rays

MARINE LIFE

Lynn M. Stone

Rourke

www.rourkepublishing.com

PHOTO CREDITS: All photos © Marty Snyderman

Title page: *A southern stingray uses its keen sense of smell to help it find hidden prey while a bar jack watches.*

Editor: Frank Sloan

Cover and interior design by Nicola Stratford

Library of Congress Cataloging-in-Publication Data

Stone, Lynn M.
  Rays / Lynn M. Stone.
     p. cm. -- (Marine life)
  Includes bibliographical references and index.
  ISBN 1-59515-441-8 (hardcover)
Printed in the USA

CG/CG-

Rourke Publishing
1-800-394-7055
www.rourkepublishing.com
sales@rourkepublishing.com
Post Office Box 3328, Vero Beach, FL 32964

TABLE OF CONTENTS

Rays

Rays are flat-bodied fishes with skeletons made of **cartilage**, like sharks. Cartilage is tough, flexible, and lightweight. It is not as hard as bone. Other fish have skeletons of bone.

Scientists have identified over 550 **species** of rays and ray-like fishes. Together, rays, skates, and certain other flat-bodied fish with skeletons of cartilage are known as **batoids**. All batoids are good swimmers, despite their unusual shape.

Rays have flat, flexible bodies and skeletons of cartilage.

The largest of the rays are mantas, also known as devil rays. They flap their great outer fins like wings, "flying" through the water. Sometimes they leap from the water.

A big manta ray dwarfs a diver.

Rays and skates of all shapes and sizes, including the yellow stingray here, are batoids.

The barb of a yellow stingray can produce a painful wound.

Stingrays are well known for the spines in their tails. The spines are sharp and may have barbed edges.

The "sting" comes from the **venom** that many of these rays store at the base of their spines.

DID YOU KNOW?

Rays use their tails to defend themselves. Ray tails may be up to 10 feet (3 meters) long in some stingrays or they may be stubby.

What Rays Look Like

A typical ray looks like a big Frisbee with a whip-like tail. The smallest rays are the size of a human palm. The largest mantas are more than 20 feet (6 meters) across and weigh more than 2,000 pounds (901 kilograms).

A typical ray has a flat, disc-like body and a long tail.

The **pectoral fins** give rays their broad, flat shape.

A ray's two eyes are on the top of its head along with two **spiracles** for breathing. The ray's mouth is underneath the head. A ray has two rows of five or six narrow openings called **gill slits** behind the mouth.

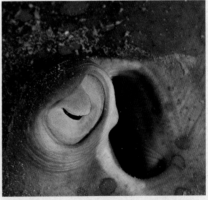

A blue-spotted ray shows the open spiracle near its eye.

The pectoral fins of rays are enlarged to form a disc shape.

Where Rays Live

Almost all batoids are **marine** fish. They live in the Atlantic, Pacific, and Indian oceans. They live in both warm and cool water, shallow and deep.

Most rays live on the sea bottom in sand or mud. Rays also live in patches of sea grass and on coral reefs.

DID YOU KNOW?

Certain species swim at depths of at least 10,000 feet (3,000 meters). Others live near the ocean surface.

A bat ray swims over an undersea garden of eelgrass.

Predator and Prey

Like sharks, rays are predators. They hunt and kill other animals for food. Most rays live on small marine animals that live in sand or mud. A few species of rays eat small fish. The manta lives largely on **plankton**.

The torpedo, or electric, ray can stun and kill prey with a charge of electricity!

A diver watches a numbfish, a type of electric ray.

A thornback ray makes a meal of squid eggs.

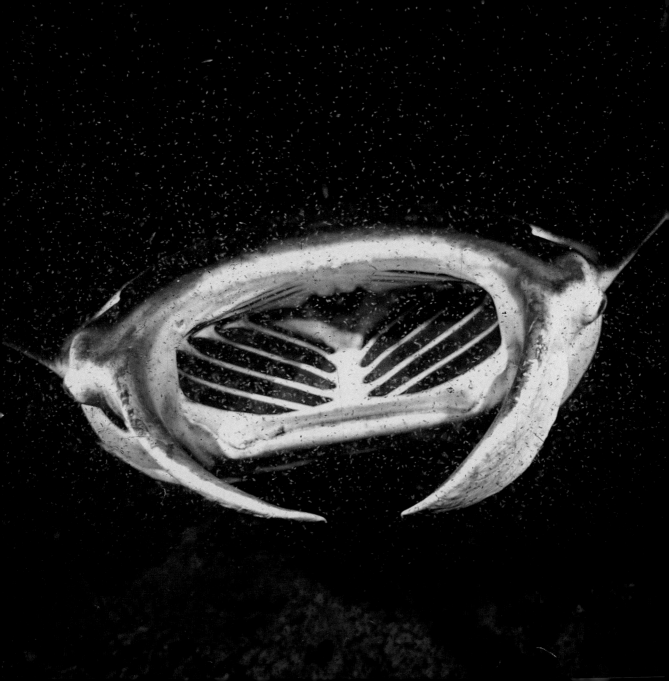

Rays have different kinds of mouths depending upon what they eat. The manta has teeth only in its lower jaw, and they are small. Skates and stingrays have strong, pointed teeth to hold prey.

The big mouth of a feeding manta strains plankton from the sea.

The Life Cycle of Rays

Baby rays are born alive. Baby skates hatch from eggs. In many skate species, the eggs are held in leathery egg cases.

In most cases, young batoids look like tiny versions of their parents. They swim freely and catch tiny prey.

This manta ray may be older than the snorkeler watching it!

Rays and People

Rays are graceful swimmers. Divers enjoy watching them. Sometimes divers feed large schools of rays.

Signs near beaches often warn swimmers and waders about stingrays. A stingray is dangerous only if someone steps on its tail. The tail spike can create a painful, but not deadly, wound.

In some countries, people take batoids for food, necklaces, and leather.

A southern stingray shares its ocean home with a diver.

Glossary

batoids (BAT oydz) — flat-bodied fish with cartilage skeletons; skates and rays are batoids

cartilage (KART ul ij) — a strong, lightweight, flexible material that forms the skeletons of sharks and rays

gill slits (GIL SLITZ) — openings to a fish's gills

marine (muh REEN) — of the ocean

pectoral fins (PEK tuh rul FINZ) — the front fins of fish

plankton (PLANK tun) — the small plants and animals that drift in the sea

species (SPEE sheez) — one kind of animal within a group of closely related animals, such as a *southern* stingray

spiracles (SPIR uh kulz) — breathing holes, such as those found in rays

venom (VEN um) — a poison produced by certain animals for defense or to kill prey

Index

Further Reading

Hirschmann, Kris. *Rays*. Thomson Gale, 2002

Websites To Visit

http://www.sdnhm.org/kids/sharks/andrays.html
http://www.unsolvedmysteries.com/usm414563.html

About The Author

Lynn M. Stone is the author and photographer of many children's books. Lynn is a former teacher who travels worldwide to pursue his varied interests.